TONGUE OF A CROW

Also by Peter Coyote:

Sleeping Where I Fall

The Rainman's Third Cure

Unmasking Our True Self

TONGUE OF A CROW

Peter Coyote

Four Way Books
Tribeca

Dedicated to the life and memory of my sister,
Elizabeth Ann West

Library of Congress Cataloging-in-Publication Data

Names: Coyote, Peter, author.
Title: Tongue of a crow / Peter Coyote.
Description: New York, New York : Four Way Books, [2021] |
Identifiers: LCCN 2021005289 | ISBN 9781945588952 (paperback)
Subjects: LCGFT: Poetry.
Classification: LCC PS3603.O976 T66 2021 | DDC 811/.6--dc23
LC record available at https://lccn.loc.gov/2021005289

This book is manufactured in the United States of America and printed on
acid-free paper.

Four Way Books is a not-for-profit literary press. We are grateful for the assistance
we receive from individual donors, public arts agencies, and private foundations.

This publication is made possible with public funds from the
National Endowment for the Arts

and from the New York State Council on the Arts, a state agency,

We are a proud member of the Community of Literary Magazines and Presses.

CONTENTS

PARIS: A LEICA AND A RAINCOAT

When I blink my eye
I pick the pocket
of your face
for whatever it might hold,
stash it in my belly
upside down.
        Too late, my dear
        to clutch your collar!
You've been assessed
and found *wanted*
by the thief of time.

PAPERY OLD LADY AT MY GREEN LIGHT

Papery old lady, blue veins
winding down strangled in her wrists
an irritating whisper
crossing Divisadero.
Young, I thought,
What does she have to sing about?
Empty of sensation
save the tick and swell
of her central crumpled muscle,
one satiric eye—
wandering bright beetle shell
imminent with hum—
hardly human the other
its winding sheet winding
up her exposed film.

Me, I had no plans to die—

SPEEDING THROUGH

I'm driving already, in the farm Jeep
beside me, the old man's potent
rifle I'm eager to use
when the hairbrush body of a woodchuck
slips past my right front tire
racing for the woods. I leap out, grab his paw,
handle on that day's fun.

Empty pasture, moon-sliver.
Inside the empty nail-keg now
a rustling, whispering
beside me in the grass.
I work the bolt
watch the long brass cartridge
jacketed bullet rise, slam it home,
click the safety, kick
the coffin over, count an unrushed ten
behind his pumping legs and fire—

He ducks, though already dead,
so his fate might pass over.
When I, villain-style,
roll the body with my boot, I wish it had.

Cruel little cowboy, never reckoned
to find breasts, each nipple leaking
mother's milk? The knowing woods,
too big to search for hungry
denned and hidden pups.

A sharp-eyed hawk cries out.
In the shadow of his circling
all my lusts go lame. Now
the hawking moon
is flecked with blood.

DO WE ALL MOURN?

Do we all mourn the childhood
steamed away like water
on a skillet? Have I lost
a favorite book?
I can't remember the title,
just the word "Esmerelda."

*

Ruth, mother of my childhood,
slapping solitaire in the after-school afternoon—
raising her lip-sticked glass—

In my bedroom closet
something lurked, every night, behind
the glow-in-the-dark star door
I made Ruth shut and rattle the handle
three times to prove it closed. My dreams
of shrieking cartoon
cats and dogs, cries
floating through the dark house, pollen,
guiding mother to my bed,
giant pale Luna moth
with sour breath.

*

Make Mommy another, darling? The Cutty Sark—

*

Roger scaled the backyard fence carrying
a rope. Enlisting my sister,
tied me to the steel swing set.
Cinching the knot tight, whispering
I'm really on your side,
runs off with Muffet and eats my lunch.

*

Morris slams the black Bakelite
phone against the desk, eyes flecked with bitterness
and his need to hurt something,
kicks Tan, my retriever, in the stomach.
What'd she do? I shout, and run—.

*

The Old Man passed out,
Demerol, standing in the open door
of the refrigerator, sweaty head slipping on the damp glass.
Potato salad and deli salmon
ripped open, untouched.
Leading him to bed, turning
the hall corner to his room, his shadow
suddenly looming.
He throws his boxer's weight behind
a punch, crushing the plaster and skeletal
lath while I tug him
to where he sleeps.

*

Was I carefree in the *back before dark*
days? I can't remember. What was that book?
Memory's a room with drawn shades,
light seeping around the edges, but
too dark to read.

Only the shine on Wendy's lips
glows, beguiling constellations of freckles,
breasts stretching her ruddy sweater
impulses gathering mass
in my jeans. Her mocking smile—
Was my body ever my own?
I can't even hide inside it.
My father's gaze now includes me
among his enemies.

Did the monster get me?
I want to read that book again.
Where did the luminous robin go
once so vivid on my emerald lawn?

EARTH IS A WOMAN, SURE

I.

Earth is a woman, sure, but
most beautiful when
rain-glistened ravens are tattooed
on the grey cheeks of the sky
and the wild geese cry
      Avalokiteshvara's pity for the passing world.

II.

To you, my friend, questioning
my lifelong addiction to women
in despair,
I can offer only the mystery of myself—
who will follow high cheekbones, long-legs
of an axe-murderess into an abattoir.
I evade the point, I know
but can't speak clearly
about the constant fog
in my mother's eyes
and what is required for me
      to remember her rare smiles.

III.

I find the earth most beautiful when it rains,
inspiring the limping, wounded rabbit in my brambles
to venture forth. Decades earlier,
in the fragrant barn loft, safe
in the blanket my father clutches
around us as if we'd survived a shipwreck.
The drumming tin shelters us
from the rain assaulting the roof—
scents of mown grass and the pear brandy
my father rubs off his chin, as if summoning
his own forgetting of the rusty nails
set in his flesh when he was my age.
His love of rain is mine.
His wife, my mother, pale as a lab rat
was stripped of her rain clothes
after my younger sister was born.
In this remembered yesterday
our lives were opposing lines
of traffic, headlight blind, on a two-lane bridge.
        My father soothes my forgetting
with his own. The heaving flank
of mountain—his chest

that crushes my mother,
and sometimes darkens and fills the doorway
of my room with threat, now sighs like a far wind.
High in the eaves
      pigeons pace and gargle
      restlessly.

THIRTIETH YEAR

On the verge of the creek's-edge field
my young dreaming
hard against the turbulent water,
boys new to long pants
trading girlie pix, Viceroy butts behind
the garage. Rods, reels,
silvery spinners shimmering out,
tempting the fish. The whip
of fiber poles, the flash
of line easy as promises to a
girl I thought was stupid.
She turned her head
to check my lips aimed at hers.
Don and Woody weren't dead
from bullets in eighth grade, released
to the muddy suck of the stream.

PERIODICITY

Three bone buttons
on my left moccasin,
full moon, half-moon, quarter.

Opening and closing on
the grassy bank—
the mouth of a large pike—
the silver moon of the lure inside,
the hook piercing its cheek.
Picked up, slammed down
next to that moccasin.
Seeing roe, reconsider
put the stunned fish back
—it breaks loose then—
writhes to the surface
the sore wound
between a woman and myself—
She's back—
a flash of white belly
rolling, pale moon eclipsed
by mossy clouds
sick dark water—

pearly bellies, mother and child.
Moonstruck in Leo
I wound mothers and am sad,

skeletons on my shoes,
a man fishing for relief
under her moon-sharpened barb.

TOXIC SUGAR

This woman—my child in her belly,
seed in a fallen apple—has fled.
Frostbitten in Jemez? Cracking
a rabbit carcass by her fire?

Her chill worms its way
into my California cabin.
My slap failed to obliterate
her scorn…

Driving from town, her hand
dancing in my fly. I brake, skid
onto the gravel shoulder.
Splayed against a phone booth
in the dark, we fuck and bite like mink.
I was never certain she could read.

Lighting my lamp
the box of matches blazed up
blistering my fingers.
There's always heat when I think of her
and tonight, licking my fingers,
I can think of nothing else.

TWO CONVERSATIONS IN CHICAGO

If these walls could talk, huh?
she gurgles conspiratorially,
maneuvering a pink suitcase
between the stainless steel jaws
of the elevator as they hiss closed.
I'm trapped in the bad air
of her soiled hair, sullen face, cheesy white plastic
belt and cheap shoes. I disguise a gasp
as preparation to speak:
These walls?
      You mean the Chicago thing?…Capone…?

She cocks her head as if inquiring
if I'm alive—
      What did you think I meant?
and the rumble of our descent appears
to emanate from her mouth as a growl.
I couldn't say
      I wasn't thinking anything.
I didn't say
      Why don't you get your teeth fixed
      or brush them?
I nearly said
      Hey, I've been demoted by divorce

of a wife I never cheated on to this shabby shit-hole hotel
and the forced confinement of an 8-floor drop
while my silence is being violated by a woman
resembling a pork chop.

I wanted to say

Couldn't we just stand here quietly
while I stare into the perfect, undistorted mirror of myself
that is you?

I WOKE WITH A WOMAN / ZAZEN

1.

I WOKE WITH A WOMAN

I woke, a woman by me
in the dark. Her breathing sharp
and I thought her lips
did something with my name.
I stumbled through that night
in a season of no moon.
And then slept again and again
until I woke up in the wrong bed,
interrogated by sunlight
and lying, lying to its face.

*

2.

ZAZEN

Ankles and thighs
acknowledge each other:
right palm defines

back of left hand.
Teeth, tongue
and palate chat
among themselves,
knee sends SOS.

In the vastness:

    rooster cry

    raspy engine bark

    thought:

    have I outlived my dick?

LONDON RUN

*—Having been flown to London by the Grateful Dead, with Ken Kesey
and company and two Hell's Angels, in 1969 to assess the Beatles' cultural
hipness and introduce the San Francisco scene to Europe*

6 December London
grey junkie pallor sky
12 to feed and house
Apple office first stop
timid George, the skinny one,
suggests a cheap hotel
"Where they take anybuddy"—
Kesey gone for days,
this morning's script croaker
his mad maiden aunt and psychotic kid
scratching and washing invisible sores
rents us a flat—room for 8
plus maiden aunt and freak—
81 Prince of Wales Mansions
sandwiched between Kensington
and Battersea bridges
shabby Funland across the road
chained for winter—
moldy furs, McVitie's biscuits
Typhoo Tea, strainer-brewed,

jacks—legal pharmaceutical heroin—
more effective than the weak heater
eating shillings,
speed-freak litter of candy bars,
squashed butts, soiled clothes
scattered around the stately manse
the sallow motherly clutter
for our brood of feral West Coast birds,
Stanley Mouse painting the tanks
of the Hell's Angel choppers
parked in the chilled foyer.

My little English Jenny Wren
her leather coat and urchin scarf
breast pale as talcum powder
brushes and ties up my hair
laughing, prodding me awake.
My loneliness for California's
damp green hills and fog.
Wish I could fly her home—
patchouli-scented Saturday
desk in a high London window

painted shut, behind me
Sweet William's eyes closed, dropping
cigarette ashes on his clothes—

"Battersea" they call it.
Battered orphans of the wars at home—
"Sea"—the sound of oceans we've crossed
in our fretful goings and comings
seeking a new world.

1972

needle wheedle
feelin' shitty?

sleep city
steel titty

heroin in the loo

POPPIES

Helen's poppy-wine libation
twice noted by Homer
for relieving the cares of men,
the drowsy flower and her knowledge
of its arts, the white milk dripping
from the scarred nipples.

My crop is in and I'm shaking
seeds from the plump, dun, pods
over a baking sheet, grains
smaller than salt,
pods for tea
on nights I can't sleep
seeds to plant for next year's doldrums.

I've scored, scraped, and smoked
the waxy sap, chased the dragon
to Spain, North Africa, Paris
and the dirt of my own gardens, minor rewards
for turning my back on the bone-white dust.
Smaller than salt,
all history and sexual delight,

scraped into a small sack, dreaming
of next autumn and the sweet cloying smoke
of my pipe rushing.

Poppy, Poppy, oh Papa—
sad shooter of Demerol
        curse, bless, me now with your fierce tears
you have fretted the strings
of my life, shortening them
raising their pitch but
never above flattened thirds.
Your pitiless onyx eyes
razored cheeks and lilac
talc, bespoke suits
talons deep in the belly
of money, your rage—
the canker on my heart
as I've been yours.

MINING WORDS

Coal releases a gassy wavering flame—
a lethal iris.

This light is steady
an opium den, a lamp of sootless olive.

STILL LIFE

Plump chair
fire of polished brass
pyramid of five nectarines
on a white plate
edged in blue.
The air washed and softened
by jasmine and rain.
The servants bowed out
door hushed closed.
The waning crescent
of my wife's sad mouth.

THE HAIRLESS CUCKOLD

My wife's cat crushed by a speeding car.
11p.m.—three beeps from the phone—.
Someone at the gate—.
Neighbor's voice: bad news.
She—listening, twisting her hands
as if the breath was sucked
from her body by the moon,
could have been the nightly news.

Floating ahead in her white robe.
to the smear where his head—.

She cried all night and did not sleep.
Three days on is still crying.
Face morphing to putty.
My little man, she moans.

Each morning before dawn.
The little rounder, the little back-door man—.
Hours in each other's arms.

"*The boop*," she'd crooned.

The dwarf in a cat suit, I thought.

The hole left can't be filled.

By me.

THE DOGS OF BUCHAREST

The dogs of Bucharest are dusted
with crumbled mansions, ash
of red flags. They doze
in ruined dreams abandoned
by their masters. They bark
whelp and die without
plan or permission. Occasionally,
like thinkers, like poets,
they are rounded up
and shot.

A bitch with flapping teats
haunts the ruined foundry
where I film diversions
for my country. Feral eyes watch
me poke a sumptuous lunch,
the roll I proffer.
She trembles, her whimpering
pups beneath a rack of iron.

Sad and sooty sumacs,
tattered sorrel, scattered
pages of a book—
It's cheap to film in ruined lands.

There's a story that the Buddha
gave his body to starving lion cubs.
The hunger of the dog—
would a better man feed her
his fingers?

THE ONLY ONE TALKING

Walking and slipping to a lunch—
a blizzard in a city where I don't live—
the snow, inhaled pepper.

Garbage men huffing into their hands
rocking from foot to foot
slapped by the wind.
Stumbling into Bubba's
I signal for coffee.

The young couple next to me
speaking French, sharing a crisp salad.
Caught observing their plates I blurt—
Il me fait rigoler que vous pourriez
mangez nourriture froid aujourd'hui.

perhaps my three rhymes
prompt her to spear a tomato slice
as if my tongue—
Why am I the only one talking?

COLD AND CLEAR

Ringed with   sighing traffic,
the marsh has   surrendered to gravity.

Today's rain a weak   asthmatic fret,
tide inhaled, the land   gasping for water.

Small silver blades—smelt—slash   the surface
snatching gnats, dimples   of insistent hunger.

It is my own   dry season.
Two ravens familiar   from daily walks

swoop and light   before me,
demanding   the peanuts I carry for them.

How charming to   think of them
as friends.   How like me

to gild   opportunism with romance.
Once I called that   marriage.

THE VIGILANT DOG

...weak man, be unwilling to chase what flees
                        —Catullus

You hate "to sleep alone. Full stop."
Husbands may not, lovers will not
dictate terms: one may buy and one may spend.
But I cannot sit and eat with you
damp from the arms of another man
with that other man. This isn't
to insist you're not yours to spend
and I would never have you lie.
But even a dog knows when
to look away and when
it's safe to return.

CHÂTEAU DE GARRAUBE

Forests are the highest organization of sunlight—to forests.
They don't begrudge the deep, slow pulse of succession—
beech, larch, and oak choked by pines—or the cumulative
heaving of leaves, mushrooms foraging on mulch and rot.

But to the men who felled and hewed the old-growth trunks—
clearing the fields to pry this house's stone from the earth's clench,
hewing true angles, blocking, winching, stacking
the ancient granite as they willed—
the axes and two-man saws made a wiggy martial music.

The stately manse, floats on a crushed granite plinth,
dominating the foaming marsh below. Its character
does not tip from true or sink beneath the ravages of lichen
and moss. Its fate, like ours, is to once again be dust,
but for now, the chambers of its heart still open and close
on hammer-dimpled hinges, creaky as a ship's rope
stretching on a pulse of tide.

The empire that launched this armada is now a sigh
of wind. The statesmen who carved Indochine and Allemagne
like racks of lamb at the great tables, are neighbors now
to stones. The lead soldiers on the attic tables once recorded

geometries of ancient feuds, now stripped of meaning as
a bird-stained statue (who's that guy?) in a South American park.

The spring still flows, the reason for the house.

The ancient crimes can't be compensated,
and a slight brown girl still serves at table.
We're a sun-ruddy and vigorous lot.
We are not afraid to laugh and laugh,
making the forest echo, under the moon of dry ice,
the moon of dry white wine.

PLACE DE LA CONCORDE

Rippled stone,
roars, grinds, whines,
blurred and sudden traffic,
motorcycle barking
over the bridge.

Then, a cascade of notes,
unnaturally loud because
a street lamp with a missing pane
houses a soot-grey sparrow
singing and singing *sans cesse*.
The song amplified,
like a drunk chanting in a tunnel,
thirsty for the company
of a voice like his own.

PLINK-PLUNK

Trees comb water
from fog
sigh, sing, play
the glistening ground
of mind.

Trees comb water
sigh, sing, play
the glistening ground
of mind

SUN OF HONEY

Preparing my daily rounds
after days of rain.
New sun climbs
the high garden wall,
piano notes
drip off ivy
each tapped leaf
a pressed key.

The still bright day
glissades and chords
two voices—
girl and man—
caress an aria.
Sudden heat on my cheek
love of this honey-sunned world.
I can't move.
Pierced by beauty
as if swarmed
by bees,
everything just
this moment
arrived.

THE EDGE OF THE SEINE, GORGED
ON SPRING RAIN

At my hotel's golden door at last
saluted by a man who nods
as if tipping his hat. A laugh makes me turn.
La Grande Roue— the enormous, bleached Ferris wheel,
in languorous twinkling orbit—half-masked
by the facades of the Boulevard.

Among the few things
I don't doubt today—its
invisible creaking and wheezing,
the flood of souls in the Metro under the cresting Seine
the begging boy's accordion,
and the Seine itself, bearing bodies
and soil and the gay lights to the bottom
of the endlessly roiling sea.

SIX COLD COMFORTS

A burglar sacks your house,
dropping a pearl necklace as he leaves.

A mugger rifles your wallet, tosses back
the picture of your ex-wife.

Slitting the tongue of a crow enables it
to speak English.

How to bring home the bacon in Bengal?
Club the baby's foot.

Protesting corruption, a man immolates himself.
Temporary relief from the cold for homeless vets.

Getting what you asked for, served on your lover's heart.
Salty gravy tears.

ATTENDING A DEATH

Her blood drowning in CO_2
the plastic-wrapped utensils
the two-cent join failed
the nurse who doubts
the puddling morphine I discover
under the dispenser by the bed
the Golem jerking the leash of her veins
"Reflex," the nurse explains, each time
she gasps and her back seizes as an arch.
My futile cooing to her
sightless shocked eyes, dialed in
to no known frequency.
An honor-guard of children surround the bed
the *Prajna Paramita* sutra,
the waved sprig of cedar picked along the grimy
Concord road. The nothing
I can do, the pitiless flexing,
belly-up, thudding back to the padded bed
the phrase "run to ground," to ground,
a pink and panicked rabbit.

Then, the lonely of all things
shoes waiting like dogs to be walked
steel hangers whisper in closets

like hostages fearing execution.
Trees, bare as electric wires,
the faded green tablecloth,
the fragile porcelain cup.

SNOW GEESE AND CROWS

small ache
in my low back.

"The cold finger of death?"
Maybe *just* an ache?

Behind the finger—
Buddha-nature.

Behind Buddha-nature
No-nature.

Behind No-nature
fat crows in the pickleweed.

WORLD ON FIRE

Tarnished silver sky
a lid on the salt marsh.

Clouds steam over the far hills
stingy with rain.

Geese, egrets, herons—
pigments smeared across the sky.

The last pelican?
The last small birds?

Each panting breath
begging the rain.

Morning's last damp hope evaporates.
A scalding ray pierces the clouds,

ignites the bush beside me,
orange berries blazing.

As if I needed reminding
the world is burning.

A CHARLEY HORSE

Elfin
lithe
nickel bright,

her smile
a catch
in my breath.

Who sleeps with dogs
three cats and
a parrot

conversational with them,
caressing, making
me covet a nest in her lap,

a dog's head, a cat's body.
an otter
at home in the water

playful, supple
lethal to shelled creatures
like myself.

BIRTHDAY CALL

Hard light, desert-sun-dawn,
flat as a gravedigger's spade,

chips of bird song flaked off
morning. Ruth-less day.

(How clever of me.)
First birthday absent a mother.

Phoning Muffet,
both of us orphans now.

I complain aloud.
She cracks her flinty laugh,

says, "Not to be pessimistic,
but odds are you've had

more birthdays with her
than you will without."

YAHRZEIT

Eighteen years since
that birthday call—
no one on the other end.

CEREMONY

Crisp as a shaman's rattle
the chitter of nuthatch and junco.
Late plums drumming the garden steps.
Mixing his mother's ashes
with birdseed, elbow-deep
in a galvanized pail,
swishing the whispering
seed with ghostly flour,
pollinating each grain
with her smoky voice and pearls.

His hands in the seed.
Her flesh a gritty surprise.

HAWK FEATHERS

The tangerine tree pregnant
with its weight of tiny suns
shades the deck, bird feeders and suet.

Television twitters from inside.

I've hung hawk feathers
on threads to deter the birds from
smashing the reflections
of trees, far hills and clouds.
But still, here's a tiny goldfinch
stunned on the boards.

I blow on it and it blinks,
set it near the water dish, on guard.
The hills, the silence of laurel,
apple blossoms plum blossoms.

Inside, the President blames
a stylish Muslim congresswoman
for 9/11. *Who will rid me
of this troublesome priest.*

The finch flaps its baby wings
twice, lofts its puffball body
into the air. Falls ten inches, clutches the thorns
of a climbing rose.

A Sharp-shinned Hawk hurtles
from within the tangerines
tearing it off into emptiness.

My children live far away.

GRINDING FINE

My blue blanket
specked with sand

my children kicked there—
even the dust mints memories.

OLEMA, WINTER

Quiet scarred kitchen
sizzling lamp wick
kerosene perfume
not one cricket, only
the beautiful girl
threading a necklace of Crow bones.
Chips of firelight dance
on my ring
new screens all around
broken panes replaced last September.

This table's names carved by many knives
four guns, each over a door
the shotgun killed four
quail with one blast—
heads drying in a paper bag
feet, crimped and stiff
in a ceramic saké cup
breasts and legs in my belly
feathers in her hair,
entrails in the blue-eyed dog.
In the first rain of winter
I shot them all together
in their little covey.

THE LITTLE BIRD

Never expected to be tracing your name
on the faint ruled line of a black-edged
altar card, even after these ten years waiting
for the matted donkey crapping in your yard
to flatten you with a kick...

A one-winged bird with no song
perched on my shoulder, the sun half-
risen over the ridge...
You've gone nowhere, I know,
but still, the clamp, the clinch
of the bird's curved claws.

3 a.m.

still dressed, in my reading chair
black cat
on my lap

black suspenders
black watch band
parallel lines
riving my body
my opinions
of myself

nose to tail
the sleek fur sack
flexes claws in my thigh.

Awake in the dark
as if I had a choice.
Some pains you put up with
some you shouldn't.

DON'T WAKE THE SLEEPER

Don't wake the sleeper
crushed bones
spits of feathers
glassy stains on the frost
Powers
imagination does not dare
Presences
    the Owl's comb feather
    black talon
    coyote's scat
    wind rattling leaves
    blown back fur

Unless you're ready, it's chancy—

Owl I sing to your black talon

Owl I sing to your yellow eye
Moon's eye is an owl's eye
—Unless you're ready—
Is a cold eye on your dreams—

OLEMA

Hardwood burns
as hot
when I have money
as when
I don't

ELECTION

Before, imagination flowered
vivid, like red cactus or

gardenias, vague in fog
in the bony skull.

This year,
stingers of bees,
thickets of agave spears,
gathering smoke.

BODHIDHARMA TRAVELED WEST

The palms on Fourth Street lean west,
tattered fronds tracking the last light
disappearing into the sea.
Why don't the palms grow straight?
The sun travels
from east to west every day—
How to account for this salute,
bowing deeply as trees are able?

THE BURNED OAK

They rooted too long during the war,
ate the tender shoots after
the forest burned,
the water fouled.

Mount a watch.
Herd what swine are left
into the rusty pen. Make a gate
from the old barn boards.
Women, whet the knives.

The oldest boy chooses,
shoots it in the head.
A .22 will do the job but
it may scream.

Force a sharpened rod
between back-leg tendon and bone
Hoist it into the burned oak.
Cut the throat.
Drain the blood into a bucket
if you can find one.

Pour scalding water down the body,
scrape the hair off the skin.
Take a sharp blade, slice the belly open,
move the organ meat to the kid's wagon.

Squeeze the guts clean, wash
for winter sausage.
We need something like a barrel
to pack what we don't eat with salt
in case the generator goes—
in case we have to fight again.

DO THE DEAD MISS US?

Is interstellar space thick
with longing?
Five senses return
to source—
"not one speck of dust"
they say, reducing reincarnation
to metaphor. Unless,
some wind-blown track,
some ghost spoor—
the stain of a pomegranate
on a crushed linen napkin—
lingers longer than we think

EQUINOX

Forty-year Zen friend,
omnisexual pre-Haight pilgrim,
has finally anchored
his rammed-earth house in the rocks
at eight thousand feet.
By the sluggish creek north of Willits
we chew through friends and lovers
flick pistachio shells
onto the murky waters, watch them
sink, sucked downstream.

SPILLED RICE

Her sack of rice has burst,
grains everywhere mixed
with dirt. Everything ruined

except the cake we ate
with our hands that last visit.
Her fearless, bone-white teeth.

The grains swirl, eddy, and drift in the mind,
become spirit—gravity-free.
Her tender fingers that banded the legs

of shrikes and falcons are now fog
brushing the schist and serpentine, rising
with the tang of *kitkitdizze* bush

vaulting over the trees.
Is she headed South
to the farm country where she grew

to shadow and cool
her kinsmen stooped in the paddies?
Is she a cloud now?

Sho Chiku Bai, Mochiko, Kokuho Rose—
Koda family sweet unsullied rice. Egrets
(I almost wrote 'regrets')

white as unopened bandages
forage the toxic soil. "Gone, gone,
gone beyond." Carol, you'll come back
as the rain.

NO JAR, NO LID

Boyhood summer
evening running
bug-jar and lid
hissing summer lawns

Years of daybreak sitting
jar and lid gone
only the winking

Here   gone
Here   gone
           "Letters from emptiness . . ."

WHERE OH WHERE

is my mother gone? My brown childhood
home now painted blue.
My black bike gone from the porch.
Doctors are younger than my daughter.
Spots on the backs of my hands, maps
of unknown galaxies. Oh
where is mother gone?
Where am I going
to meet her?

EXHALATION

A spider
sleeps at the gates of sense
the breeze—scent of olive—
stopped
the gate
ajar
a gasp for air
in a grove of roses
rattles
a black and yellow bird
an echo impaled on thorns.
The gate
prevents nothing—
in or out.

Notes

"Toxic Sugar" is for Sam; "Poppies" is for my father, Morris; "Mining Words" is dedicated to Peter Koch and the Extraction Project. "Château de Garraube" is for Mark and Susie Buell; "The Vigilant Dog" is for Katharina. "Sun of Honey" for the late Judithe Bizot; "A Charley Horse" for Jody; "The Little Bird" and "Birthday Call" are for my late sister, Elizabeth Ann West; "Don't Wake the Sleeper" is for Jim Koller; "Equinox" is for Paul Shippee; "Spilled Rice" for the late Carol Koda; "Exhalation" is for Robert Duncan.

I am particularly grateful to Brenda Hillman for her early support and encouragement, without which these poems would never have been revisited and revised. My friend, fellow Zen priest and fine poet Peter Schireson led me to Patrick Donnelly, my editor and painstaking mentor. His acuity, respect for form, abhorrence of sentimentality and sensitivity to nuance, helped me transform a drawer stuffed with 55 years of foolscap and scribbles into this book. My gratitude to Martha Rhodes for her support, her eagle-eyed edits and for creating and maintaining Four Way Books. Blame the pandemic for her not receiving full, in-person prostrations. These four people are as responsible for whatever excellence here as I may be. I'll accept sole ownership of gaffes and flaws. I would like to add that three poems originally intended for collection were pulled from publication honoring the request of an ex-wife. In concurring, the Buddhist priest overruled the artist.

"Poppies": "curse, bless, me now" alludes to Dylan Thomas's "Do Not Go Gentle into That Good Night."

No Jar, No Lid," the line "hissing summer lawns" is remembered from James Agee's *Let Us Now Praise Famous Men*.

The poems in *Tongue of a Crow* were written between 1964 (when Peter Coyote came to California to study for an MA in Creative Writing with Robert Duncan) and extend to the present day. Mr. Coyote has authored three previous books—a memoir of the counter-culture years, *Sleeping Where I Fall* (Counterpoint Press, 1999), a chapter of which, "Carla's Story," won a 1993/94 Pushcart Prize. Mr. Coyote's second book, *The Rainman's Third Cure* (Counterpoint Press, 2015), was nominated for best creative non-fiction in that year. His latest, *Unmasking Our True Self* relates Zen practice to actor's training in mask and improv work to engender liberated states. It will be published in Fall of 2020 by Inner Traditions.

Mr. Coyote supported himself as an actor, performing for many distinguished filmmakers, in a career of over 150 films, including Barry Levinson, Roman Polanski, Pedro Almodovar, Steven Spielberg, Martin Ritt, Steven Soderberg, and Sidney Pollack. He has narrated an equal number of documentaries including eleven directed or produced by Ken Burns. He won an Emmy for *The Pacific Century*, by Alex Gibney in 1992 and a second for his narration of Mr. Burns' *The Roosevelts: An Intimate History* in 2014.

In 2011, after studying Zen Buddhism for 37 years, Coyote was ordained as a Zen Buddhist priest and in 2015 received "transmission" (independence from his teacher's authority). He makes his home on a small farm in Northern California with 40 fruit trees, makes jam and sleeps with his two dogs—*los vatos locos*—Chico and Pablo. He considers his most intractable addiction to be his 1952 Dodge Power Wagon.

Publication of this book was made possible by grants and donations. We are also grateful to those individuals who participated in our 2020 Build a Book Program. They are:

Anonymous (14), Robert Abrams, Nancy Allen, Maggie Anderson, Sally Ball, Matt Bell, Laurel Blossom, Adam Bohannon, Lee Briccetti, Therese Broderick, Jane Martha Brox, Christopher Bursk, Liam Callanan, Anthony Cappo, Carla & Steven Carlson, Paul & Brandy Carlson, Renee Carlson, Cyrus Cassells, Robin Rosen Chang, Jaye Chen, Edward W. Clark, Andrea Cohen, Ellen Cosgrove, Peter Coyote, Janet S. Crossen, Kim & David Daniels, Brian Komei Dempster, Matthew DeNichilo, Carl Dennis, Patrick Donnelly, Charles Douthat, Morgan Driscoll, Lynn Emanuel, Monica Ferrell, Elliot Figman, Laura Fjeld, Michael Foran, Jennifer Franklin, Sarah Freligh, Helen Fremont & Donna Thagard, Reginald Gibbons, Jean & Jay Glassman, Ginny Gordon, Lauri Grossman, Naomi Guttman & Jonathan Mead, Mark Halliday, Beth Harrison, Jeffrey Harrison, Page Hill Starzinger, Deming Holleran, Joan Houlihan, Thomas & Autumn Howard, Elizabeth Jackson, Christopher Johanson, Voki Kalfayan, Maeve Kinkead, David Lee, Jen Levitt, Howard Levy, Owen Lewis, Jennifer Litt, Sara London & Dean Albarelli, David Long, James Longenbach, Excelsior Love, Ralph & Mary Ann Lowen, Jacquelyn Malone, Donna Masini, Catherine McArthur, Nathan McClain, Richard McCormick, Victoria McCoy, Ellen McCulloch-Lovell, Judith McGrath, Debbie & Steve Modzelewski, Rajiv Mohabir, James T. F. Moore, Beth Morris, John Murillo & Nicole Sealey, Michael & Nancy Murphy, Maria Nazos, Kimberly Nunes, Bill O'Brien, Susan Okie & Walter Weiss, Rebecca Okrent, Sam Perkins, Megan Pinto, Kyle Potvin, Glen Pourciau, Kevin Prufer, Barbara Ras, Victoria Redel, Martha Rhodes, Paula Rhodes, Paula Ristuccia, George & Nancy Rosenfeld, M. L. Samios, Peter & Jill Schireson, Rob Schlegel, Roni & Richard Schotter, Jane Scovell, Andrew Seligsohn & Martina Anderson, James & Nancy Shalek, Soraya Shalforoosh, Peggy Shinner, Dara-Lyn Shrager, Joan Silber, Emily Sinclair, James Snyder & Krista Fragos, Alice St. Claire-Long, Megan Staffel, Bonnie Stetson, Yerra Sugarman, Dorothy Tapper Goldman, Marjorie & Lew Tesser, Earl Teteak, Parker & Phyllis Towle, Pauline Uchmanowicz, Rosalynde Vas Dias, Connie Voisine, Valerie Wallace, Doris Warriner, Ellen Doré Watson, Martha Webster & Robert Fuentes, Calvin Wei, Bill Wenthe, Allison Benis White, Michelle Whittaker, and Ira Zapin.